Baptism

The Believer's
First Obedience

Larry E. Dyer

kregel
PUBLICATIONS

Grand Rapids, MI 49501

Baptism: The Believer's First Obedience

© 2000 by Larry E. Dyer

Published by Kregel Publications, a division of Kregel, Inc., P.O. Box 2607, Grand Rapids, MI 49501. Kregel Publications provides trusted, biblical publications for Christian growth and service. Your comments and suggestions are valued.

For more information about Kregel Publications, visit our web site: www.kregel.com

Unless noted, Scripture quotations are from the New American Standard Bible © the Lockman Foundation 1960, 1962, 1963, 1968, 1971, 1972, 1973, 1975, 1977.

Scripture quotations marked KJV are from the King James Version of the Holy Bible.

Library of Congress Cataloging-in-Publication Data
Dyer, Larry.
Baptism: the believer's first obedience / Larry Dyer.
    p.   cm.
Includes bibliographical references.
  1. Baptism. I. Title.
BV811.2.D94   2000   234'.161—dc21   00-035728
                                   CIP

ISBN 0-8254-2497-6

Printed in the United States of America
1 2 3 / 04 03 02 01 00

To Donna, my beloved wife,
constant companion,
blessed helpmate,
and loving friend,
with gratitude
for your support,
encouragement,
and inspiration

Contents

Preface

Water baptism for believers in Christ was instituted by our Lord. It has been the visible initiation ritual of the church for nearly twenty
centuries. Jesus commanded it; the apostles practiced it. But what does it mean? Many people are
confused about baptism, wondering, "Why should
I be baptized?" "Is baptism a requirement for salvation?" "How should baptism be practiced?" "Is
it ever right to be rebaptized?" Such questions
demand answers.

This book is designed to help those who are
preparing to be baptized. It will also help those
who want to understand baptism better.

Each of the first four chapters is designed to
answer one of the central questions relating to
the subject. Chapter 5 looks at practical issues

that arise in studying the issue, and chapter 6 addresses theological questions. Chapter 6 particularly answers those who assert that there is no salvation apart from water baptism.

1

What Is Baptism?

Five types of baptism are mentioned in the New Testament, though only two of the five have to do with water. No wonder people become confused. It is necessary, when reading Scripture, to stop at each occurrence of the word *baptism*. Ask, "What kind of baptism is referred to in this text?" The five baptisms are:

1. John the Baptizer's water baptism
2. Christian water baptism
3. Jesus' baptism, which was His suffering on the cross
4. Jesus' baptism of believers with the Holy Spirit
5. Jesus' baptism of unbelievers with fire

John's Water Baptism

> Then Jerusalem was going out to him, and
> all Judea, and all the district around the
> Jordan; and they were being baptized by
> him in the Jordan River, as they confessed
> their sins. But when he saw many of the
> Pharisees and Sadducees coming for bap-
> tism, he said to them, "You brood of vipers,
> who warned you to flee from the wrath to
> come? Therefore bring forth fruit in keep-
> ing with repentance." (Matthew 3:5–8)

John was known simply as "the Baptizer"
(Matt. 3:1). He came as an Old Testament prophet
in the deserts of Judea, baptizing in the Jordan
River north of the Dead Sea. The Bible only
records that he baptized Jews as a sign of repentance for their sins. Repentance was a spiritual
preparation for receiving the coming Messiah
(Christ). By demanding water baptism of the children of Abraham, who saw themselves as the holy
"people of God," John testified that spiritually
they were no better than Gentiles, from whom
they had demanded proselyte baptism for hun-
dreds of years. (A proselyte is a Gentile convert
to the faith of Israel.)

At the time Jesus Christ came to be baptized,
Jews were actively seeking to bring Gentiles into
the Jewish faith through proselyte baptism. The
meaning of water baptism was clear to all Jews,

and people throughout Israel came to be baptized by John in the Jordan River.

This symbolic act demanded by John was centuries old. Near the south entrance to the ancient Jewish temple, archeologists have excavated remnants of cleansing *miqwaot* baths. At Qumran these baptismal baths have one set of stairs leading into the water and a separate set of stairs for those who had finished ritually cleansing themselves, so that they would not touch those who were unclean by mistake. In Jerusalem, the *miqwaot* would have been visited by pious Jews on their way to the temple to worship.

Outward physical immersion expressed an inward spiritual repentance, in preparation for the Messiah's coming. But when the Pharisees and Sadducees came to John for baptism, he charged that their behavior did not demonstrate true repentance.

By demanding water baptism of the children of Abraham, who saw themselves as the holy "people of God," John testified that spiritually they were no better than Gentiles.

The water baptism John practiced had purposes beyond that of expressing individual repentance. It was the way God wanted John to manifest the Messiah to Israel. As John baptized the repentant Jews, he was looking for the Messiah. Although John knew Jesus as a human being, he did not know Him to be the Christ until Jesus came for baptism—until he saw the confirming signs from God:

"And I did not recognize Him, but in order that He might be manifested to Israel, I came baptizing in water." And John bore witness saying, "I have beheld the Spirit descending as a dove out of heaven, and He remained upon Him. And I did not recognize Him, but He who sent me to baptize in water said to me, 'He upon whom you see the Spirit descending and remaining upon Him, this is the one who baptizes in the Holy Spirit.'" (John 1:31–33)

Christian Water Baptism

No one can be baptized today with John's baptism. His baptism was only for the Jews and anticipated the coming of Christ. Technically, we do not *follow the Lord* in water baptism. The baptism Jesus received was not Christian water baptism. Jesus was baptized in a Jewish rite of preparation for His own coming.

We *obey the Lord* by submitting to His command to be baptized. John's baptism is distinct from water baptism in Jesus' name. John 4:1b–2 records that Jesus instituted this practice during his earthly ministry: "Jesus was making and baptizing more disciples than John (although Jesus Himself was not baptizing, but His disciples were)." Once the prophet John had declared Jesus to be the Messiah, Jesus began to gather His own following. For a short time, both John and Jesus were at the Jordan River, making and baptizing disciples. John would make disciples and point them to Jesus, who would take them beyond John's teaching.

> After these things Jesus and His disciples came into the land of Judea, and there He was spending time with them and baptizing. And John also was baptizing in Aenon near Salim, because there was much water there; and they were coming and were being baptized. For John had not yet been thrown into prison. (John 3:22–24)

The Pharisees tried to provoke John to jealousy and get him to criticize Jesus, but John's answer surprised them. "He must increase, but I must decrease" (John 3:30). John was perfectly happy to point others to the Savior, rather than attempt to gain a following for himself. As people deserted John for Jesus, they were rebaptized in the name of Jesus to identify themselves as His followers. Jesus used the same rite of initiation that John had used. Once individuals had expressed faith in Jesus, they were immersed in water by one of His disciples.

An incident in the city of Ephesus years later helps distinguish John's baptism from Christian baptism. In what is today western Turkey, Paul found Jewish disciples of John the Baptizer. Apparently, they had made a pilgrimage to Israel about twenty years before, during John's ministry. At that time they had recognized his prophetic ministry and submitted to baptism in the Jordan. Then they returned home to await the Messiah. They never heard the news that the Christ had come. They did not understand that the Messiah had died, was resurrected, and had ascended to heaven. Neither did they know of the outpouring of the Holy Spirit upon the church.

Technically, we do not follow the Lord in water baptism. . . . We obey the Lord by submitting to His command to be baptized.

And it came about that while Apollos was at Corinth, Paul having passed through the upper country came to Ephesus, and found some disciples, and he said to them, "Did you receive the Holy Spirit when you believed?" And they said to him, "No, we have not even heard whether there is a Holy Spirit." And he said, "Into what then were you baptized?" And they said, "Into John's baptism." And Paul said, "John baptized with the baptism of repentance, telling the people to believe in Him who was coming after him, that is, in Jesus." And when they heard this, they were baptized in the name of the Lord Jesus. (Acts 19:1–5)

John's baptism was preparatory for Jews awaiting the coming of the Messiah. All those who were baptized in water by John had to be rebaptized in water when they identified with Jesus Christ as their Savior. This is the Christian baptism we practice today.

Jesus' Baptism of Suffering on the Cross

Jesus used baptism to refer figuratively to His suffering in Mark 10:38: "But Jesus said to them, 'You do not know what you are asking for. Are you able to drink the cup that I drink, or to be baptized with the baptism with which I am baptized?'" Jesus was calling His upcoming crucifixion a "baptism." He viewed His crucifixion as an immersion in suffering.

Jesus' Baptism of Believers with the Holy Spirit

John predicted that the Messiah was the one who would baptize believers in or with the Holy Spirit: "And he was preaching, and saying, 'After me One is coming who is mightier than I, and I am not fit to stoop down and untie the thong of His sandals. I baptized you with water; but He will baptize you with the Holy Spirit'" (Mark 1:7–8). After His resurrection, Jesus confirmed to His disciples John's words of promise.

> And gathering them together, He commanded them not to leave Jerusalem, but to wait for what the Father had promised, "Which," He said, "you heard of from Me; for John baptized with water, but you shall be baptized with the Holy Spirit not many days from now." (Acts 1:4–5)

The baptism of the Spirit followed just ten days after Jesus' ascension to heaven from the Mount of Olives. At that time, Jesus sent the Holy Spirit into the hearts of believers. It was called the baptism of the Holy Spirit because the believers were immersed by the Holy Spirit into the spiritual body of Christ, which is the church. The church was formed by the Holy Spirit's coming on the Day of Pentecost. Thus, with this baptism of the Holy Spirit, a new community, the church was begun, in which the Holy Spirit united all believers and placed them within the body of Christ. The baptism of the Spirit is referred to frequently, but it is only once defined. In 1 Corinthians 12:13, the apostle Paul teaches that Spirit baptism is the possession of every believer:

For even as the body is one and yet has many members, and all the members of the body, though they are many, are one body, so also is Christ. For by one Spirit we were all baptized into one body, whether Jews or Greeks, whether slaves or free, and we were all made to drink of one Spirit. (1 Cor. 12:12–13)

The Baptism of Fire

Baptism is used figuratively in Scripture to refer to the coming judgment. In Luke 3:16–17, John predicted that all his Jewish audience would experience the Messiah's baptism. Either they would believe the One who was coming and experience the baptism of the Holy Spirit, or they would reject Him and experience the baptism of fire in judgment. While some have seen the *baptism of fire* as a reference to the Holy Spirit and to the tongues of fire on the day of Pentecost (Acts 2), the context of John's words imply judgment; he is condemning the unrepentant Pharisees. *Fire* speaks of the judgment that will fall upon those who do not bring forth the fruit of repentance. The vivid New Testament picture of judgment is that of the Messiah on a threshing floor, separating the wheat from the chaff and burning the chaff with unquenchable fire.

And the ax is already laid at the root of the trees; every tree therefore that does not bear good fruit is cut down and thrown into the fire. As for me, I baptize you with water for repentance, but He who is coming after me is mightier than I, and I am not fit to remove His sandals; He will baptize you with the Holy Spirit and fire. And His winnowing fork is in His hand, and He will thoroughly clear His threshing floor; and He will gather His wheat into the barn, but He will burn up the chaff with unquenchable fire. (Matt. 3:10–12)

A respected reference work for pastors and laypeople, *The New Bible Dictionary*, agrees. It tells us that two Old Testament writers compared God's judgment to a stream of God's fiery breath (Isa. 30:27) or to a river of fire (Dan. 7:10).[1] Those who refused to repent and accept John's baptism would face a terrible future "baptism by immersion" in that river of fire when the Messiah came.

One issue remains: If the Bible says there is "one Lord, one faith, one baptism" in Ephesians 4:5, how can there be five? As far as the church of Jesus Christ is concerned, there is ultimately only one baptism that unites us spiritually into Jesus Christ and connects us to one another. That is the baptism of the Holy Spirit. Water baptism is the outward picture of this inner spiritual baptism (1 Cor. 12:13).

Of the five baptisms mentioned in the New Testament, one denotes Jesus' own suffering on the cross. See the table below for a comparison of the other four. Jesus performs real baptism of believers in the Holy Spirit. He will baptize unbelievers with the fire of judgment at the end of the age.

Two baptisms, the baptism of John and baptism in the name of Jesus, are symbolic and use the medium of water. John's baptism was a preparation for Christ's appearance, whereas Christian water baptism is public identification with Christ. John baptized Jewish people, but all believers in Jesus receive Christian baptism.

The baptisms of Jesus are in themselves spiritually effective while Christian water baptism is not spiritually effective to produce salvation. It symbolizes the Spirit's baptism.

	Element	Meaning	Subjects	Significance
Baptism by John	Water	Preparation for Christ	Jews only	Symbolic
Christian baptism	Water	Public identification with Christ	Believers	Symbolic
Baptism by Jesus	Holy Spirit	Personal union with Christ	Believers	Spiritually effective
Baptism by Jesus	Fire	Final judgment	Unbelievers	Spiritually effective

The Meaning of Baptism in the New Testament

2

What Does Christian Water Baptism Mean?

Christian baptism is "an initiatory washing with water in the name of the Father, the Son, and the Holy Spirit," according to Paul Jewett, "which the risen Lord commissioned His apostles to administer to all His followers as a mark of their discipleship."[1]

The central text for establishing this task is Matthew 28:19–20. It is commonly called Jesus' Great Commission of the church: "Go therefore and make disciples of all the nations, baptizing them in the name of the Father and the Son and the Holy Spirit, teaching them to observe all that I commanded you; and lo, I am with you always, even to the end of the age."

The main command is to "make disciples." The apostles are to make disciples by baptizing them and teaching them. In the Great Commission, baptism is the rite of introduction into discipleship. Baptism publicly sets apart those who believe the gospel. Jewett explains:

> Baptism, then, is an outward symbol of an inward spiritual transformation. From God's viewpoint it is an outward sign to those who believe that their sins have been washed away by the blood of Christ and they have been united with Him by His Spirit in His new resurrection life. It is a sign to one being baptized that he is a full partaker in all the benefits and blessings which Christ has secured for believers. On the believer's part, baptism is a public repentance for his sin and confession of his faith in Jesus Christ as his Savior. As well it is a sign of his discipleship; that he is giving himself up to Christ to walk in the transformed life commanded in the Gospel.[2]

God's Pledge to the Believer

Forgiveness of Sin

Baptism is a reenactment, an outward picture or symbol of what God has done in the life of the believer through faith. Water baptism, therefore, is the result, not the cause, of regeneration. This is Peter's reasoning in Acts 10:44–47:

> While Peter was still speaking these words, the Holy Spirit fell upon all those who were listening to the message. And all the circumcised believers who had come with Peter were amazed, because the gift of the Holy Spirit had been poured out upon the Gentiles also. For they were hearing them speaking with tongues and exalting God. Then Peter answered, "Surely no one can refuse the water for these to be baptized who have received the Holy Spirit just as we did, can he?"

The baptism of the Spirit was the saving act that came first. Water baptism followed as the outward sign of the Holy Spirit's inner work in the lives of these Gentiles. This is the norm for believers. Spiritual regeneration always occurs prior to water baptism, because it is associated with the moment of faith. According to Peter, faith in Christ qualifies us to receive the ordinance of water baptism.

Baptism publicly sets apart those who believe the gospel.

Peter was preaching to the first Gentile congregation at Cornelius's house. While he was still speaking, the Holy Spirit fell upon all who heard the message. This was an unexpected, supernatural act of spiritual regeneration. The entire group apparently believed Peter's message and was immediately saved as he spoke. Peter had not even finished speaking, when the entire congregation was instantly converted.

The gift of speaking a language these Gentiles had never learned was given to them as a one-time sign for the sake of the skeptical delegation of Jews. God gave them unmistakable proof that He accepted Gentiles on the basis of their faith in Jesus Christ, just as He did the Jews. The gift of speaking in unknown languages was proof positive that regeneration had occurred in these Gentiles' hearts, and that the Holy Spirit had been given to them. Without a visible sign, the Jews present would not have known what had taken place. Note Peter's response in Acts 10:47. "Surely no one can refuse the water for these to be baptized who have received the Holy Spirit just as we did, can he?" Since they had received the Holy Spirit in regeneration, they were qualified to receive water baptism as the outward sign and token of their new inward relationship with God. The new believers were ordered, not "asked," to be baptized.

The waters of baptism indicate the spiritual washing or cleansing of the heart. Paul uses this metaphor to describe the inner transformation of the Corinthian believers. They had been caught up in the grossest immorality. They were covetous swindlers. "But you were washed, but you were sanctified, but you were justified in the name of the Lord Jesus Christ, and in the Spirit of our God" (1 Cor. 6:11b). Water baptism reenacts the complete cleansing from sin that occurs at the moment of personal faith in Christ. It assures the believer of the promise of God. It is a pledge of God's forgiveness.

Identification with Christ

Water baptism pictures the baptism of the Holy Spirit, which identifies the believer with Jesus Christ (see table, p. 19). At the moment of faith we are spiritually baptized into Christ. Paul explains that this union with Christ has grand implications.

> Or do you not know that all of us who have been baptized into Christ Jesus have been baptized into His death? Therefore we have been buried with Him through baptism into death, in order that as Christ was raised from the dead through the glory of the Father, so we too might walk in newness of life. (Rom. 6:3–4)

From the moment of regeneration, the old sinful nature is no longer the supreme power in life. Christians have spiritually died with Christ, been buried with Christ, and have risen to a new sphere of life with Christ. From now on they are to live in the power of Christ for the glory of God. Water baptism pictures all of this. The great spiritual transformation described here can only refer to the work that the Holy Spirit does when a person believes in Christ. Water baptism itself cannot do this. Water baptism illustrates identification with Jesus Christ, but the Spirit's baptism is what accomplishes it.

Baptism by immersion accurately depicts this inner spiritual transformation. Descending into the water indicates the believer's death with Christ to the old way of life. Being covered over with water symbolizes burial with Him. Ascending from the water proclaims that the new Christian's life will never be the same. Paul says that "our old self was crucified with *Him,* that our body of sin might be done away with, that we should no longer be slaves to sin; for he who has died is freed from sin" (Rom. 6:6–7).

Union with Christ

Water baptism illustrates more than an identification with His death, burial, and resurrection. It signifies that the believer has been spiritually plunged into Jesus Christ by the Spirit. The act of immersion pictures the spiritual immersion of the believer into the body of Christ.

First Corinthians 12:13 describes the baptism of the Holy Spirit. "For by one Spirit we were all baptized into one body, whether Jews or Greeks, whether slaves or free, and we were all made to drink of one Spirit." Spiritual union with Christ is the basis for every other spiritual blessing. Only because they are *in Him* do God's people possess "every spiritual blessing in the heavenly places" (Eph. 1:3). Immersion pictures, if only briefly, that permanent union with Christ that entitles the believer to share in His everlasting glory.

The act of immersion pictures the spiritual immersion of the believer into the body of Christ.

So, water baptism signifies a pledge from God that He has accomplished three acts of transformation in the believer's life:

1. spiritual washing from sin
2. identification with Christ in His death and resurrection
3. union with Christ, which brings every spiritual blessing.

The Believer's Pledge to God

With water baptism, believers also make three statements before God and other people. First, Christians declare their personal repentance of the sins that have characterized their lives. Second, they confess that Christ is the only Lamb of God, who takes away the sin of the world. Third, the disciples accept the commitment to be loyal followers of Jesus.

A Declaration of Repentance

Normally people bathe because they are dirty. Symbolic washing and cleansing imply the presence of sin. Baptism is a public renouncing of past wickedness and rebellion. Baptism is a profession of repentance, a change of mind about sin in which we are declaring that we have repented of sin and desire to turn from it. Baptism is closely associated with repentance in Acts 2:38 and in the ministry of John the Baptizer (Mark 1:4; Luke 3:3; Acts 13:24; 19:4).

A Public Confession of Faith

Since water baptism is the God-ordained means by which believers acknowledge faith in Christ, baptism in the name of Jesus functioned from the earliest days of the church as the *rite of entry* or initiation into the new sect of those who called upon the name of Jesus (Acts 2:21, 41; 22:16; cf. Rom. 10:10–14; 1 Cor. 1:2).[3]

To be baptized "in the Name of the Father, Son, and Holy Spirit" is to be identified with the Trinity. It is a way of saying that you believe Jesus, the Son of God, is as divine as the Father and the Spirit.

Baptism publicly identifies a person with Jesus Christ, marking the Christian as "Christ's one."

> For I do not want you to be unaware, brethren, that our fathers were all under the cloud, and all passed through the sea; and all were baptized into Moses in the cloud and in the sea; and all ate the same spiritual food; and all drank the same spiritual drink, for they were drinking from a spiritual rock which followed them; and the rock was Christ. (1 Cor. 10:1–4)

Receiving baptism in a man's name links you to that person. That is why Paul is adamant that people should not say they were baptized in his name (1 Cor. 1:13–15). He wants them linked only to Christ. Water baptism identifies the person being baptized as a follower of the one whose name is invoked. When Israel passed through the Red Sea under Moses' leadership, all Israel was baptized into Moses. Symbolically they were identified as followers of him. Of course, only the Egyptians actually got wet. This experience at the Red Sea is called a baptism, because it separated the Israelites forever from their past lives and masters. The experience dedicated them to the God who led them by the cloud. Baptism is always a separation from the old life and a commencement of the new.

Faith in Christ means that the old life of sin is

forever behind, and a new life of obedience has begun. Baptism means identification. Christian baptism separates the followers of Jesus Christ from all other masters.

A Declaration of Loyalty

Water baptism indicates a pledge of loyalty to Christ. It commits the believer to discipleship. In the first century, accepting baptism put the life of the convert on the line. He was saying, "I am a follower of a crucified king." Such a confession might bring punishment from the authorities. Baptism should be understood as pledging no less a loyalty than that today.

Christian baptism separates the followers of Jesus Christ from all other masters.

Since submitting to baptism proclaims personal death in reference to sin, it is, in fact, a statement before the believing community that "I am re-deemed. I am changed. You can expect all the rest of my life to demonstrate that change." Thus, bap-tism demands a life of discipleship in the Savior's footsteps. Once the baptized disciple has identi-fied himself with the believing community, fellow believers can hold him to his commitment. In fact, they have a responsibility to support him and to demand that he be accountable.

Some professing Christians refer to water baptism as a sacrament. The word comes from the Latin *sacramentum*, which means both "a thing set apart as sacred" and "a military oath of obedience as administered by the commander."[4] Certainly, baptism is one of two sacred ordinances given by our Lord Jesus to the church, the other being the Lord's Supper. Viewed in this light, water baptism has been given by the commander, the Lord Jesus, as a way for the Christian to affirm a decision to follow Him and suffer with Him in the call of duty. Only in that sense can baptism be called a sacrament.

A Symbol, Rather Than a Sacrament

The sacramental understanding of baptism has been the source of much confusion and error. The concept of sacrament underlies all infant baptism. Baptism should be referred to as an ordinance rather than a sacrament because, as Charles Ryrie says, "It does not incorporate the idea of conveying grace but only the idea of a symbol." Believers' baptism requires a responsible decision on the part of the person being baptized. The believer must personally exercise faith in Jesus Christ. Naturally, this precludes infants, who have not reached an age at which they can exercise personal faith and obedience.

Those who hold a sacramental understanding

of baptism vary greatly in what they mean by the term. The Roman Catholic view is that baptism is a means by which God imparts saving grace. As Protestant apologist H. Wayne House explains, "In RCC [Roman Catholic Church] theology, baptism takes away all sin, original sin, and all personal sins as well as punishment for sin. Baptism also restores sanctifying grace to the soul."[5] Faith is not required on the part of the infant because the rite, when properly performed, is sufficient to save the child if he or she should die in infancy. House observes, "One should not understand from this RCC teaching that the faith of the adult person is excluded in the act of baptism, only that it is not 'an efficient cause of grace.'"[6]

While most do not go so far as the Roman Catholic Church, other groups offer this sacramental theology as well. Orthodox godparents or sponsors make a statement of repentance and faith on the infant's behalf. Unlike Roman Catholics, the Orthodox do not see the Holy Spirit at work in the child until a separate confirmation sacrament, *Chrismation*. Somewhat illogically, in defending infant baptism as a Christian rite, Orthodox theology identifies it with the pre-Christian baptism performed by John for repentance in expectation of the Christ. *Chrismation* is identified with the reality of the coming of the Holy Spirit at Pentecost. Yet baptism is also called a "new birth by water and the Holy Spirit," a personal Easter.[7]

Baptism is a proclamation of the individual's personal faith in Jesus Christ and of the inward work of the Holy Spirit.

Lutherans, like the Roman Catholics and the Orthodox, closely connect the work of the Holy Spirit with baptism, though it is thought to convey grace only to those who believe. Paul Enns states, "The Lutheran view is that faith is a prerequisite. Infants should be baptized and may possess unconscious faith or faith of the parents."[8] Lutheran theology rightly recognizes that the infant is unable to volitionally understand and believe. Since faith is a gift of the Holy Spirit, the Church assumes that God grants faith to the child at the point of baptism, though the child is unaware of it personally. Those who take such a view, of course, stand in direct contradiction to the theology of grace alone through faith alone in Christ alone expressed by Martin Luther.

Reformed and Presbyterian churches view the sacrament of baptism as a sign and seal of the covenant of grace. Though he does not take the position, Millard Erickson succinctly explains the Reformed understanding when he says that "Sacraments are not the means of grace . . . by virtue of some inherent content of the rite itself. . . . But like circumcision in the Old Testament, baptism makes us sure of God's promises."[9] For further discussion of infant baptism and the relationship between salvation and baptism, see pages 63–70.

The Bible teaches that the grace of God is received through faith, not baptism (Eph. 2:8–9). Baptism *proclaims* regeneration but does not produce it. Baptism must never be viewed as a human work that adds to or completes salvation. Rather, baptism is a proclamation of the individual's personal faith in Jesus Christ and of the inward work of the Holy Spirit. Perhaps enough confusion has arisen around the word *sacrament* that it should be avoided altogether.

So water baptism is an outward sign of an inward relationship. It is like a wedding ring which, although it is not necessary for marriage to occur, is still an important symbol of the vow of commitment that unites a couple. Likewise, baptism is a symbol of the transforming work of God in the hearts of those who believe.

3

Why Be Baptized?

The New Testament offers two reasons for baptism: First, it is an act of personal obedience, and, second, it is a profession of faith. Water baptism is commanded by our Lord for all His followers (Matt. 28:19). It was practiced consistently by the apostles. We submit to baptism out of personal obedience to the Lord. Water baptism also is the God-ordained means of professing our faith. Often, though not always, it took place publicly in the New Testament. At least one other Christian must be present to administer baptism, and usually there are many others present, so it is also a witness.

Seven Common Objections

In Acts 8:36 an Ethiopian court official asked Philip the evangelist a classic question, "What prevents me from being baptized?" Philip's response indicated that nothing stood in the way. Unfortunately, that is not the case for many today. At least seven misunderstandings prevent people from being baptized.

1. Isn't water baptism optional?

Water baptism is commanded by our Lord for all who claim His name (Matt 28:19). The Great Commission commands those who make disciples to baptize them. All believers in Jesus are to be baptized. Likewise, Jesus' commission in Mark underscores the importance of this command. "Go into all the world and preach the gospel to all creation. He who has believed and has been baptized shall be saved; but he who has disbelieved shall be condemned" (Mark 16:15–16). At first glance, the passage seems to make salvation conditioned upon baptism. This is not so. The second half of the verse points out that belief is the issue. Clearly, however, water baptism is expected to accompany belief. As stated above, baptism is depicted in the New Testament as the outward demonstration of inward faith. Faith is impossible to see; it must be manifested in a concrete, identifiable way. Jesus commanded water baptism as a way of making faith evident. For further discussion of Mark 16:15–16, see pages 72–73.

The apostles' practice demonstrates that they took Jesus' commands seriously. Water baptism naturally follows profession of faith in the book of

Acts. This can be seen on the day of Pentecost, during which three thousand were baptized (Acts 2:41).

In Acts 8:35–36, as soon as the court official understands the message of the gospel, he wants to be baptized to indicate his acceptance of that message. He does not ask for baptism with the idea that being dipped in water automatically brings salvation. But right at the point where, today, some might ask a person to "pray a prayer and receive Jesus Christ as Savior," Philip baptizes the Ethiopian. Baptism, in conjunction with a confession of faith, is the New Testament way to profess faith in Christ.

Baptism is depicted in the New Testament as the outward demonstration of inward faith.

The idea of an unbaptized believer is foreign to the New Testament. Simon believed and was baptized (Acts 8:13). Saul followed his initial faith in Jesus Christ with baptism (Acts 9:18). Cornelius, the Roman centurion, received water baptism subsequent to faith (Acts 10:47–48). The experience of Lydia is normative:

> And a certain woman named Lydia, from the city of Thyatira, a seller of purple

fabrics, a worshiper of God, was listening; and the Lord opened her heart to respond to the things spoken by Paul. And when she and her household had been baptized, she urged us, saying, "If you have judged me to be faithful to the Lord, come into my house and stay." (Acts 16:14–15)

Her heart was opened by the Lord in faith, and she received water baptism. The salvation of the Philippian jailer also illustrates the biblical pattern:

And they said, "Believe in the Lord Jesus, and you shall be saved, you and your household." And they spoke the word of the Lord to him together with all who were in his house. And he took them that *very* hour of the night and washed their wounds, and immediately he was baptized, he and all his household. (Acts 16:31–33)

In the jailer's case, water baptism was administered immediately, in the middle of the night, probably because of the tense political situation. The pattern was the same in Corinth: "And Crispus, the leader of the synagogue, believed in the Lord with all his household, and many of the Corinthians when they heard were believing and being baptized" (Acts 18:8). Jewish disciples in Ephesus were baptized in response to faith in Christ (Acts 19:3–5).

From all the New Testament evidence, we conclude that water baptism is the divinely appointed expression of faith in Christ. It is commanded by Christ Himself, practiced by the apostles, and is therefore not optional for the believer.

Pastors must not hold back new converts from baptism. These passages contradict the practice of intentionally delaying the baptizing of new believers. There is no New Testament support for a period of verification between one's profession of faith and the act of baptism. In fact, the evidence suggests that baptism should be performed as soon as possible. Proper instruction of the convert should precede baptism, but there is no biblical precedent for putting off baptism until converts demonstrate fruit.

2. Baptism seems like a religious tradition that has no relation to my Christian life.

If baptism has lost its meaning, the church needs to recover it. Baptism is an act of separation from the past and identification with Christ before the world. Orthodox Judaism may understand this better than do many Christians. If an Orthodox Jew accepts baptism, the family may hold a funeral for that person, who will be forever after regarded as dead. A Jewish person can pray as a follower of Christ, attend Christian meetings, or read the New Testament and face relatively mild disapproval. But let the Jewish Christian take the step of baptism, and the Jewish community may

cut him off.[1] They understand baptism better than
do some Christians. They recognize it as a definite act of separation from the past and identification with Jesus Christ. In a Muslim country
baptism always means persecution and may mean
death. Baptism marks the believer's rejection of
past beliefs. It means adopting the way of Christ.

Baptism is not just a tradition. It is a meaningful sign of identification with Christ and with
the rest of His body. It is a rite of initiation for
those whom God has received. Why shouldn't
anyone be baptized who wants to be identified as
a Christian?

3. I was baptized as an infant, so I don't need to baptized again.

This objection arises from a misunderstanding. Water baptism is not a means of conferring
the grace of God on our children or insuring their
salvation. Some baptized infants grow up to demonstrate rebellion rather than regeneration. One
of the greatest errors we could make is to depend
upon our "baptism," as if a religious ritual could
regenerate us.

There are no examples of infant baptism in the
New Testament. The closest we have are "household baptisms." Every person whose baptism is
recorded in the New Testament *believed first*. It is
a tragedy to take the clear New Testament teaching of believers' baptism and use it as a rationale
for infant baptism followed by confirmation.

Infant baptism arises from a theological argument that lacks scriptural support. Parents in Scripture dedicated their children to God, but none had them baptized. Those who believe that infant baptism is an extension of the Old Testament covenantal rite of circumcision argue that the New Testament includes only examples of conversions from paganism, and not of the children of believers. Evidence to the contrary should not be so easily dismissed.

Beyond scriptural concerns, the practice of infant baptism often subtly undermines a covenant child's ability to perceive the need for a personal conversion to Christ. This is especially true when parents and churches do not follow through with the obligations on which covenant baptism is built. There is a tendency to look forward to some sort of customary Christian education program that "confirms" in the juvenile the vow the parents and church made on his or her behalf in infancy. It can be a cultural rite of passage into adulthood. Many adults believe they are saved simply on the basis of long-ago ceremonies that meant little or nothing to them and were attended by no personal repentance and turning to the Savior.

The biblical order is profession followed by baptism. Therefore, this is the sequence that should be followed. Not only is it the biblical pattern and the sequence commanded by Jesus Christ, but it also encourages a better understanding of salvation. It nurtures a lifelong attitude of thankfulness to Christ as the only ground for our salvation.

4. I am afraid to be baptized, because it will offend my family's religious beliefs.

Some may avoid baptism because it would hurt the feelings of parents who had them baptized as infants. We return to the great danger of people trusting in rites to save them. Parents may indeed be displeased that a child is baptized as a believer, and the reason could be that they do not themselves trust in Christ for their own salvation. Such people desperately need to see the truth, and they will see it best through the witness of those they love.

By refusing to take the step of believers' baptism, the new Christian may unintentionally signal to family that what has occurred is not a radical new birth. The believer who wants to be baptized can say, "I am a different person than I was before I expressed belief in Jesus. I appreciate my parents' desire to commit me to God as a child. God has honored that. Now that I personally believe in Christ, I want to express that faith by personal obedience to the Lord's command. Infant baptism does not do that."

That may be an offensive message to relatives who believe that their own infant baptism places them in a relationship with God. It communicates that they need to be spiritually born again.

Soman Varghese was born in South India and

baptized as an infant in the Syrian Orthodox Church. In keeping with the Orthodox understanding of baptism, he believed that his infant baptism had conferred special blessings and that, as a result of it, he had always been a Christian. When he came to the United States to study, he heard the pure gospel presented for the first time and realized that he needed to be born again to have a true spiritual relationship with Jesus Christ. His testimony to his parents of that event is a model:

> I was saved in the fall of 1985. All that year I considered baptism and its implications. Finally, as the fall of 1986 approached, I agreed to obey the Scriptures. I remembered how my parents used to criticize people who were rebaptized. Now I had to explain my decision to my parents. Even as I dialed their number in India, I feared the possibility my family would disown me. But I was willing to take that risk because I believed it was the right thing to do, according to the Scriptures.
>
> I told them, "I am not getting baptized to become a Christian but to show to the rest of the world that I have chosen to follow Christ. Salvation is through faith in Christ alone."
>
> I was telling them they were wrong. They understood, but they were still hurt.

Two years later at Christmas, while visiting them in India, my mother begged me, with tears, to come back to the Orthodox faith and denounce this baptism and the idea of being born-again. Although she pleaded with me, I stood firm. "No, I am sorry," I said, "I must follow Christ."[2]

The baptized believer can say, "I am a different person than I was before I expressed belief in Jesus."

Ultimately, this is a loyalty issue. Anyone who is convinced that Jesus Christ commands the baptism of believing adults, yet defers to family wishes, has not given full loyalty to Jesus as Lord. Jesus warned, "He who loves father or mother more than Me is not worthy of Me" (Matt. 10:37a). This issue is perhaps seen most clearly in unbelieving families or where Christians are actively persecuted. Converts from Islam, for example, are rightly questioned harshly by their fellow Christians if they refuse Christian baptism because it would offend their parents; their stand demands ultimate loyalty to Christ. Should someone who comes from a background in which Christ is named but perhaps not believed in do anything less than be biblically baptized?

5. Baptism by immersion is a public embarrassment. I do not wish to be humiliated.

There are those who have a problem with the idea of being lowered into the water publicly, because they have a problem with personal pride.

I have often wondered why Jesus chose baptism as the sign of identification with His kingdom. One reason was the existing Jewish practice of proselyte baptism, by which Gentiles were joined to the people of God during the period between the Testaments. Another reason for baptism is its symbolism. Baptism by pouring or sprinkling water on the head illustrates, in part, the pouring out of the Holy Spirit into the new believers' life (Isa. 44:3; Joel 2:23, 28–29). Baptism by immersion powerfully pictures our union with Christ and our identification with His death, burial, and resurrection.

Baptism by immersion, like repentance, is a purposeful blow to human pride and dignity. It is messy. It is not as fashionably elegant as baptism by sprinkling. To be baptized by a few drops of water while wearing a best dress or a suit and tie is so much more dignified. But to wade into a public pond or lake and be publicly dunked? This, perhaps, contributes to the reason behind Paul's statement that not many noble come to Christ (1 Cor. 1:26). Jesus said that a person enters the kingdom in childlike humility. The Lord places a premium on lowliness, for God is opposed to the proud but gives grace to the humble (James 4:6).

The Ethiopian government official in Acts 8 was an important man. He was the secretary of the treasury of his nation—a sophisticated, cultured, and educated political leader. Upon hearing the gospel, he was enthusiastic to profess faith through baptism. He seemed to be more concerned about pleasing the Lord than maintaining his status in the eyes of his attendants.

6. I can't be baptized, because I can't live the Christian life.

This objection has the ring of sincerity. Some want to take a stand for Christ but recognize the ethical and moral demands of that life and fear they cannot meet them. The person with this fear is right. No one lives a perfectly Christ-centered life, and no one dies to sin without the Holy Spirit's strength. It is not simply difficult; it is impossible. From the moment of the individual's new birth, the Spirit, who lives within, enables the Christian to begin to die to sin and live to righteousness (see Rom. 6:1–13). In fact, water baptism signifies this very victory of union with Christ.

Romans 6 confronts this issue and teaches that the Christian can overcome the power of sin through three steps:

1. Know that you have died and have risen with Christ (vv. 3–10).
2. Accept this new relationship as a radical, continuing process of dying and living (v. 11).

3. Consciously nurture an attitude of presenting your life, in its totality, to God (vv. 12–13; cf. Rom. 12:1–3).

The person who fears that Christ's standards are unattainable should make sure that this uncertainty does not camouflage a refusal to obey. Perhaps an inability to conquer sin is related to disobedience and a refusal to be baptized. A fear of being baptized can come from a lack of trust in the living Christ to enable one to overcome sin.

Perhaps the problem is an unwillingness to forsake a secret sin. For the person who claims Christ as Savior, this sin will already be destroying fellowship with God and stealing joy. True joy will come with repentance and victory over the power of sin, and public baptism signifies that very victory in Christ. It is the experience of many Christians that obedience to Christ in baptism helps enable obedience in every other struggle.

7. I have accepted Christ as Savior, but I am not ready to acknowledge Him as Lord of my life.

People who bargain with God lose. Some refuse baptism because they want to live by their own rules and simply use Christ to stay out of hell. Such a calculating attitude is frightening, for salvation is offered on God's terms or not at all. It is dangerous to say, "I'll take the free salvation, but

I'll run my life, thank you." Paul makes it clear that we can have sin or the Savior, but not both.

When we come to Christ, it must be unconditionally. We see our need and throw ourselves upon His grace and mercy. Heaven and hell are real; nothing else matters. If we are not concerned about sin, then Christ's love has not overwhelmed us. Do we know Christ at all, in that case?

Summary

The answers to all of these objections are simple. Baptism isn't optional; it is commanded by the Lord Jesus for all His followers. Far from being a mere tradition, baptism is an act of personal obedience and witness. Since the Bible presents baptism as a conscious expression of faith, it is still appropriate for a person who was baptized as an infant to express his personal faith in this way.

If we defer baptism out of a fear of offending relatives and friends, are we not being disloyal to Christ? If we refuse baptism out of embarrassment or pride, what do we say to the Savior who died that we might live? If fear of failure in the Christian life keeps us from baptism, do we not need to obey and trust God to keep His promise that the Holy Spirit will provide us with the power to overcome sin? If we spurn baptism because we do not want to submit to Christ as Lord, should we not question the adequacy of our love for the Savior?

4

What Is the Mode of Baptism?

The mode of baptism practiced in the New Testament seems to be immersion. This is supported both by the definition of the word *baptize* and by example. *Baptism* is directly related to a Greek word; it has been imported into the English language. Normally this might be done by translators because no other word is equivalent. One can argue, however, that the word *baptism* is not needed, for another word fits quite well. If the word were to be translated by an appropriate word that matches the meaning in the original, translators would replace *baptism* with *immersion*.

The Greek verb *baptizō* actually means "to dip, or to immerse." When used in the Greek middle voice it means "to dip oneself, or to wash." In non-Christian literature it occurs with such meanings as "plunge, sink, drench, or overwhelm."[1] In one occurrence in classical literature, the verb was used to describe the sinking of a ship. Why didn't the editors simply translate it that way?

Perhaps church tradition dictated the decision. If baptism had been translated "immersion," how could the practice of child-sprinkling have been justified?

The Greek prepositions in Acts 8:38–39 imply immersion: "And he ordered the chariot to stop; and they both went *down into* the water, Philip as well as the eunuch; and he [Philip] baptized him. And when they came *up out* of the water, the Spirit of the Lord snatched Philip away; and the eunuch saw him no more, but went on his way rejoicing" (emphasis added). The only reason that both of them would have needed to go down into the water together is to provide sufficient depth for Philip to immerse the court official. If sprinkling was the means of baptism, why could Philip not have used an available water skin or dipped his hand in a cup of water?

Some argue that the two of them stepped into a small flowing stream where Philip dipped his hand and sprinkled the new convert. They then stepped up out of the water together. The argument ignores the usual meaning of *baptism*. There is no validity to the argument that the waters could not have been deep enough for immersion. This incident occurred on the road from Jerusalem to Gaza, which passed water sources. It did not occur in the desert around Gaza. One source that fits the context was only four miles from Jerusalem.[2]

Baptism by Pouring

There is some evidence that pouring was used as a mode of baptism very early in church history. According to the *Didache* (second century), baptism by pouring three times upon the head was practiced if immersion was not possible. Immersion was still the predominant method.[3] Pouring may have been allowed in cases of extreme illness, or when water was not available. Christian drawings in the catacombs show candidates standing waist-deep in water while the one doing the baptizing pours water over their heads from a vessel he holds.[4]

A case can be made from the Old Testament for baptism by pouring. Pouring great quantities of water on the head pictures the pouring out of the Holy Spirit as He comes into the new believer's life (Isa. 44:3; Joel 2:23, 28–29). But there is no New Testament support for sprinkling as a mode of baptism. Since the meaning of the word implies immersion, it seems best to baptize by immersion.

The Formula

Matthew includes a different formula for baptism from the book of Acts. Matthew 28:19 mentions baptism "in the name of the Father and the Son and the Holy Spirit." In contrast, four times in the book of Acts, baptism is done in "the name

of the Lord Jesus" (Acts 2:38; 8:16; 10:48; 19:5).
This is not really a contradiction, since one includes the other. To baptize in the name of the
Trinity is to include the name of the Lord Jesus
Christ. The name of Jesus is the distinctive as-
pect of the Trinitarian formula. Such a baptism
identifies one with Christ the Mediator and the
God-Man. The deity of the Father and the Spirit
was not in question. At issue was the deity of the
man, Jesus of Nazareth.

5

Practical Hints for Baptism

It can be a frightening prospect if your church requests that you give a verbal "testimony" of salvation at the time of baptism. A testimony in a courtroom is simply the statement by the witness of the facts. When Christians speak of giving a testimony, they mean the same thing. Speaking in front of others can be intimidating, but it is also a rewarding experience.

The person giving witness of God's work need only answer three questions:

Telling God's Grace

1. What was my life like before I became a Christian?
2. How was I drawn to saving faith in Christ?

3. How has Christ changed my life since I trusted in Him?

Life Before I Knew Christ

You need not dwell on the details of past sordid behaviors. Simply admit that you were in a lost condition. Someone saved as a child can focus on how the Holy Spirit brought reminders of sin even at a young age. Those saved as teens or adults can remember the feelings of insecurity, guilt, or unfulfilled longing.

How I Became a Christian

Relate how God brought you to Himself. This is your story, so simply tell what happened to you, even if it happened at a young age or so gradually that details are difficult to state precisely. Anyone can, plainly and honestly, describe how God worked. This story need not be dramatic; it should simply be personal. Were there key events that led to a conviction of sin? Did other individuals provide a witness. They may be named, if appropriate. It is very encouraging to the body of Christ to hear how a Christian's witness led another to faith.

Since unbelievers may be present at your baptism, be sure to include the major facts of the gospel, avoiding words that only Christians really understand. Here is an example:

As Jeff shared *The Four Spiritual Laws* booklet with me, I understood for the first

time why I did not have a relationship
with God. I had always felt guilty, but
pushed it away. Now I was face-to-face
with the fact that I *was* guilty of evil
thoughts and actions. If I died, then I
would be cut off from God forever. But God
loved me and sent Jesus Christ to take
my punishment by dying on the cross in
my place. Then He came back from death
so I can have victory over death in Him. I
wanted that Savior. I bowed my head and
put my faith in Jesus Christ alone to save
me from sin.

How Christ Has Changed My Life

What difference has conversion made to you?
Is there assurance of forgiveness and confidence
in eternal life, rather than the former fear of
death? What changes have there been in your
behavior, attitude, vocabulary, and desires? Is
there love in your heart for God's Word and a desire to see things from God's perspective? Answers
to such questions add meaning to a testimony.
The testimony might continue this way:

> I had no emotional experience, except the
> deep relief that God had forgiven me. I
> immediately began to devour the Bible;
> it opened up to me as never before. I saw
> Jesus in a new light, and as I prayed, He
> made Himself known to me through His

Word. My whole life changed. Now Christ is the center of my life, and I am committed to living for Him. I have a desire to follow Him and to obey Him for the rest of my life.

God is often pleased to use baptism as a means of bringing others to Himself.

It is a good idea to write out the testimony. Refine the wording, practice it, and time it. This is an opportunity to tell unsaved friends and family members about what life in Christ is all about. Even someone who seems disinterested in the gospel may be curious about baptism or may want to attend out of friendship. This is an ideal setting for evangelism. God is often pleased to use baptism as a means of bringing others to Himself.

The Fear of Speaking

Speaking before people can be a terrifying experience. Not everyone is gifted in public speaking. You do not need to be. If you write out your testimony, you can read it if you must. There is no shame in saying, "I'm not much of a public speaker, so I will read what I have written."

If even the thought of reading in front of a group seems an impossible challenge, someone else can read the testimony. You can merely answer the brief questions your pastor asks you in front of the assembly. These questions might include:

1. Do you publicly profess by this baptism that you are trusting Jesus Christ to save you from your sins?
2. Do you wish to be baptized, in obedience to the Lord, as a public profession of your faith in Him and your desire to follow Him?

It is far easier for us to speak of God's mercy, in front of a supportive group of friends and fellow Christians, than it was for our Lord to confess His faith before the hostile crowd. Remember that when He stood before Pontius Pilate He made a good confession (1 Tim. 6:12–13). In the presence of those who despised Him, Jesus boldly confessed His identity as the Christ and Son of God (Luke 22:70; 23:3). We who claim His name should be willing to confess our allegiance to Christ, who died in our place. After all that Jesus suffered on our behalf, is it so much for us, in turn, to confess His name before others?

What to Wear

Some churches provide a garment to wear during the baptismal immersion. If a large white gown is worn over other clothing, it is a good idea to remove air pockets that may be trapped inside the fabric by pressing it against the body when entering the water. Otherwise the gown may act as a balloon and cause embarrassment. White robes add a pleasing uniformity to a baptism and suggest a formality.

Other churches prefer that those being baptized dress in washable street clothes. Do not wear only a swimsuit, for modesty is important. Baptism is a spiritual experience that should give no offense or cause for another Christian to stumble. Dress also sets the experience apart, for at almost no other time in life do we get into water fully dressed. Keep in mind that white garments may be revealing when wet. Dark clothes work best for modesty. Do not wear eyeglasses or wigs that may be lost, detracting from the spiritual focus of the moment. On the other hand, it usually is permissible for a friend or relative to take pictures of the baptism. Churches should allow and even encourage the taking of photographs. They will be meaningful reminders later on.

In my own congregation at the Chapel of the Lake, baptisms occur in the lake. At a beach or lake, I encourage those being baptized to wear heavy socks or tennis shoes that will not be damaged by water. Protection for the feet is important where rocks lie unseen on the bottom. Ask relatives to bring towels. Don't forget the camera because pictures of your baptism will be treasured for years to come.

Other Ways to Assist

Facing Fear

The fear of water or of being lowered under the water is nothing to be ashamed of. It will help the person who administers the baptism to know of such fears in advance. An experienced pastor can help quiet fears. It should help you to realize that the person doing the baptism can be trusted to know what to do, and the submersion will last only a moment.

Being Prepared for the Water

Whether the water is in a baptismal tank or at the beach, it will probably be cooler than the surrounding air temperature. To avoid making an audible gasp, proceed slowly enough into the water to become acclimated to it. On some surfaces slipping may be a danger, and there should be someone nearby to help. While the bottom of the lake or pond will almost certainly be chosen with safety in mind, those assisting should inform the person of potential problems. If there is any uncertainty about the bottom of the lake or pond, move slowly enough to feel the bottom *before* placing weight on a foot. A surprise slip can mean an unexpected plunge.

At the Moment of Baptism

The water probably will be about chest high. The pastor will give instructions in advance. You may be asked to fold your hands in front, as in prayer, or to fold your arms over your chest. This position allows the one lowering you to keep a more solid hold. It is particularly appropriate to fold your hands as you silently pray in the moments before baptism. The pastor or elder will place one hand on your arms and the other on your back. A baptismal declaration will be made, such as, "(Name), upon your profession of faith in the Lord Jesus Christ, I baptize you in the name of the Father, and of the Son, and of the Holy Spirit. Amen."

Water baptism is a deeply spiritual experience. Be much in prayer before the event.

At that moment it is important to be relaxed and wait to follow the pastor's lead. When it is time to enter the water, relax your knees, letting them bend, while keeping your feet firmly planted. The pastor or elder will most likely lay you gently back until water rushes over your head, then lift quickly. Holding your nose is unnecessary and looks unseemly. If you request it, the one baptizing can place a handkerchief over your nose, but this makes the task of lowering and raising slightly more cumbersome. It is sufficient to exhale gently during the moment beneath the water.

Weight is seldom an issue. The body's natural buoyancy enables even a small, weak pastor to baptize someone much larger.

Spiritual Preparation

Water baptism is a deeply spiritual experience. Be much in prayer before the event. Set aside the prior evening or that day for concentrated prayer. Study key passages on baptism. Perhaps you might want to use this book as a study guide on the significance of baptism. Since you are undergoing baptism to please and obey the Lord, your understanding and agreement with the Bible's texts is important.

6

Crucial Questions About Baptism

Proponents of infant baptism face a serious problem. There is no doubt that in the New Testament faith is the requirement for entrance into the Christian life, and faith is to be confessed in water baptism. The universal pattern of the New Testament is hearing the message, believing the message, and then being baptized. In order to justify infant baptism, this biblical order must be reversed to being baptized, hearing, and believing.

What About Infant Baptism?

Those who insist on infant baptism support this view in several ways. First, there is the argument from silence. Household baptisms in the New Testament might have also included infants (Acts

10:47–48; 16:15, 29–34; 1 Cor. 1:16; 16:15). One theological dictionary that supports infant baptism presents it this way:

> To be sure, there is no direct command to baptize infants. But there is also no prohibition. Again, if we have no clear-cut example of an infant baptism in the NT, there may well have been such in the household baptisms of Acts, and there is also no instance of a child of Christians being baptized on profession of faith.[1]

Scripture simply does not tell us whether there were infants in the households mentioned, but the texts do mention that the household members heard the word and believed:

> And they said, "Believe in the Lord Jesus, and you shall be saved, you and your household." And they spoke the word of the Lord to him together with all who were in his house. And he took them that very hour of the night and washed their wounds, and immediately he was baptized, he and all his household. And he brought them into his house and set food before them, and rejoiced greatly, having believed in God with his whole household. (Acts 16:31–34)

The real problem for infant baptism is the insistence in the New Testament on *believers' baptism.* Those who have believed are to be baptized—and no one else. The fact that God deals with families in both the Old and New Testaments does not imply that everyone in the family is converted.

Second, proponents of infant baptism contend that Christ said not to hinder children from coming to Him. This argument also rests upon conjecture. Paul J. Achtemeier explains the reasoning:

> Although adults were generally baptized, there is a suggestion in Mark 10:13–16 that infants were also baptized. The argument rests on the Greek term "hinder" which may have been part of the technical terminology of baptism: Jesus tells his disciples not to *"hinder"* the children from coming to him; compare the language of the eunuch in Acts 8:36 who asks, "what is to prevent my being baptized?"[2]

Paul Jewett, professor at Fuller Theological Seminary, counters this argument, observing, "It may be granted that Jesus gave his blessing to infants and little children, but this hardly seems to imply that they should be baptized. It is one thing to bring children to Christ that He may bless them; it is another to bring them to the fount."[3]

It is too great a stretch of biblical interpretation to derive infant baptism from the passages where Jesus invited children to come to Him and receive His blessing. Water baptism, according to the biblical evidence, belongs to *believers alone*. Certainly children, even young children, may believe. When they do, they should be instructed and baptized.

The third and central argument for infant baptism comes from the covenantal system of theology. Those who practice infant baptism justify it on the basis of the Old Testament covenants, beginning with Abraham. They believe that the New Testament church is a continuation of the nation covered under the Abrahamic covenant. It is a spiritual Israel. God made a covenant with Abraham and his seed that continues up to today. As Millard Erickson states the view, "Since the Old Covenant remains in force, its provisions still apply. If children were included in the covenant then, they also are today."[4] This sacramental view equates Christian water baptism with Jewish circumcision. Baptism is, therefore, an act of faith in the work of God, not by the one being baptized, but by the parents and the congregation, who promise to faithfully rear the child in the faith. One critical text on which this theology rests is Colossians 2:11–12: "In Him you were also circumcised with a circumcision made without hands, in the removal of the body of the flesh by the circumcision of Christ; having been buried with Him in baptism, in which you were also raised up with

Him through faith in the working of God, who raised Him from the dead."

The sign of baptism belongs only to the spiritual children of Abraham (believers), not the physical children of believing parents.

Covenant theology says baptism is equivalent to circumcision, as a sign and seal of the covenant. Advocates for infant baptism affirm that, for the same reasons Jews circumcised their infants, Christians are to baptize theirs. Jewett points out a subtle inconsistency in this argument. While Jews only circumcised males, Christians insist that the covenantal sign has been expanded in Christ so that all children should receive baptism. Therefore, they are not totally analogous. Further, circumcision was a physical sign for spiritual descendants, while baptism to covenantalists is a physical sign for spiritual descendants. The New Testament teaches that a person becomes the seed of Abraham by faith, not heredity. The sign of baptism belongs only to the spiritual children of Abraham (believers), not the physical children of believing parents.[5] Only believers should be baptized.

In fact, Colossians 2:11–12 speaks about the

transformation accomplished by the Holy Spirit's baptism, rather than baptism in water. We are spiritually circumcised at the same moment we are baptized by the Holy Spirit into the body of Christ.

One text sometimes used by those in favor of infant baptism is 1 Corinthians 7:14. The idea is that infants of believers should be baptized because they are "holy." "For the unbelieving husband is sanctified through his wife, and the unbelieving wife is sanctified through her believing husband; for otherwise your children are unclean, but now they are holy." Jewett responds, "If holy means such children are candidates for baptism, then the unbelieving spouse who is sanctified [same word] should also be allowed baptism."[6] As Geoffrey W. Bromiley writes:

> Those who practice infant baptism must reinterpret baptism. In their view, "baptism [of infants] is not a sign of repentance and faith on the part of the baptized. It is not a sign of anything we do at all. It is a covenant sign . . . of the work of God on our behalf which precedes and makes possible our own responsive movement."[7]

This view completely reverses every piece of evidence we have on the practice of baptism in the New Testament. If baptism were a sign of the covenant that made salvation possible, Paul should have been baptizing infants instead of merely preaching! He could never have said what he did in 1 Corinthians 1:17: "For Christ did not send me to baptize, but to preach the gospel, not in cleverness of speech, that the cross of Christ should not be made void."

Those who were baptized as infants have strong reasons for being immersed in believers' baptism once they come to personal faith in the Lord Jesus.

Because of its rejection of dispensationalism, the covenantal view fails to adequately distinguish between Old Testament Israel and the New Testament church. Baptizing infants sends the wrong message. It conveys the concept that grace is provided through a ritual act, which later must be confirmed. It can even create a false assurance in those who trust in their baptism rather than in the Savior. Such a misunderstanding is serious, for it fails to look to faith as the requirement for salvation. There is no compelling reason to practice a ritual so entirely absent from the New Testament, so opposed to its pattern, and so likely to obscure the need for personal faith in Christ.

What if I Was Baptized Before Accepting Christ?

As stated above, those who were baptized as infants still have strong reasons for being immersed in believers' baptism once they come to personal faith in the Lord Jesus.

What is the biblical pattern? How does the Bible present baptism? If baptism in the New Testament is always *believers' baptism,* then, in order to obey the Lord fully, we must be baptized as believers. Baptism by immersion is a significant event in the life of a believer who publicly takes a stand for Christ. While a Christian can still appreciate the interest and prayers of parents, nothing can take the place of a personal profession of faith and commitment to the Lord Jesus. Being baptized according to the biblical guidelines is an act of obedience to the Lord.

But another dilemma must be faced even in churches that practice believers' baptism. Sometimes a person has been baptized prematurely upon a supposed profession of faith in Christ. Genuine conversion came later. The person's life now shows the repentance and dramatic growth in the fruit of the Spirit that should follow conversion. Should there be a rebaptism? Scripture neither commands nor prohibits a second baptism. Theologically, the baptism of the Holy Spirit comes but once. Practically, however, if a believer does not feel confident that he or she has obeyed the commands of the Lord in baptism, there is no biblical reason not to be rebaptized. It seems better to err on the side of obedience than to risk disobedience.

What About Baptism for the Dead?

There is a single text of Scripture that mentions baptism for the dead. As an aside, in Paul's argument for the resurrection in 1 Corinthians 15, verse 29 says, "What will those do who are baptized for the dead? If the dead are not raised at all, why then are they baptized for them?" Careful study of these verses in the larger context of 1 Corinthians and what is known about Corinth makes it clear that Paul was alluding to a pagan practice with which the Corinthians were familiar. He certainly was not referring to Christian practice. Paul does not say, "we Christians" or "you Christians," but "they." The fact that pagans—almost certainly in the context of the popular mystery religions—baptized for the dead suggested to Paul that even some pagans believed in a physical resurrection to come. Paul doesn't approve of the practice; he simply mentions it in passing. We must not build any Christian doctrine or practice around obscure references such as this.

What About Baptismal Regeneration?

A few groups within Christianity come dangerously close to endowing the waters of baptism with a magical power to save. Some nondiscriminating members of those denominations are misled into believing that a ritual can be their ticket

to everlasting life. Other groups teach that one
cannot be saved without it, even after accepting
Christ as Savior. Such views misinterpret passages in the New Testament.

Texts Supposedly Relating Baptism to Salvation

In examining these texts to see what they do
teach about salvation, we quickly see that baptism is a witness to salvation—not its cause.

> And He said to them, "Go into all the world
> and preach the gospel to all creation. He
> who has believed and has been baptized
> shall be saved; but he who has disbelieved
> shall be condemned." (Mark 16:15–16)

Some dismiss the last twelve verses of Mark
16 as a later addition to the text, but the vast
majority of manuscripts include them. This is one
version of Jesus' Great Commission to His disciples. Literally, the text reads, "The one who believes and has been baptized shall be saved." The
Greek construction closely links the words "believed" and "baptized."

This does not make baptism an additional *requirement for salvation*. What this verse omits is
as important as what it includes. The second part
of the verse states that unbelief is the basis of condemnation. It is the lack of genuine faith that re-
sults in condemnation, not the lack of the rite of

baptism. What about the person who believes but is not baptized? Jesus doesn't imagine that scenario. Baptism is *the New Testament way of expressing inward faith in Jesus Christ*. That is why Jesus so intimately linked the act with believer's faith.

Some interpret Acts 2:38 to mean that both repentance and baptism are necessary requirements for salvation.

> And Peter said to them, "Repent, and let each of you be baptized in the name of Jesus Christ for the forgiveness of your sins; and you shall receive the gift of the Holy Spirit." (Acts 2:38)

The problem with this view is that elsewhere Scripture makes it quite clear that eternal life is promised on the basis of faith alone (for example, John 3:16, 36; Rom. 4:1–17; 11:6; Gal. 3:8–9; Eph. 2:8–9). The same Peter who preached these words on the Feast of Pentecost, promises forgiveness on the basis of faith alone in Acts 5:31; 10:43; 13:38; and 26:18.[8]

Forgiveness is based upon true repentance, and baptism follows, for the one who repents, as the sign of faith and the result of forgiveness.

There are alternative interpretations that do justice to the text. The first takes the preposition *eis* ("for") to mean "because of" or "on account of." According to this view, Peter is telling the Jews to repent and be baptized because they have received forgiveness of sins rather than *to obtain* forgiveness. While this is not the normal use of the preposition *eis*, it does occur elsewhere. In Matthew 3:11, for example, John the Baptizer says, "I baptize you with water *because of (eis)* your repentance" (author's translation). John's baptism was not designed to produce repentance but to express it. Matthew 12:41 is a second example. "The men of Nineveh shall stand up with this generation at the judgment, and shall condemn it because they repented at *(eis)* the preaching of Jonah; and behold, something greater than Jonah is here." Nineveh repented "because of" or "on account of" Jonah's message. In the same way, Peter could be offering baptism to the people who were hearing him *because* their repentance would bring forgiveness of sins.

A second, more likely, interpretation treats the phrase "and let each one of you be baptized, every one of you in the name of Jesus" as a parenthesis. The meaning would then be: "repent [in order to receive forgiveness of your sin] and let each one of you [who repents] be baptized in the name of Jesus Christ for the forgiveness of your sins." The Greek grammar suggests it. The verb "repent" is plural, as is the pronoun "your" in the phrase "forgiveness of your sins." The two belong together. The command to "be baptized" is singular and fits with "each one of you." Forgiveness is based upon true repentance, and baptism follows, for the one who repents, as the sign of faith and the result of forgiveness. This agrees with Luke 24:47 and Acts 5:31.

Jesus' words to Nicodemus are also frequently misunderstood: "Unless one is born of water and the Spirit, he cannot enter into the kingdom of God" (John 3:5).

Some believe Jesus here refers to the waters of baptism, though that is not the most natural interpretation of these words in their context. While speaking to Nicodemus, a teacher in Israel, Jesus insisted that "unless one is born again, he cannot see the kingdom of God" (John 3:3). The Greek word that often is translated "born again" can mean "born from above," as well as "born a second time." Nicodemus incredulously asked if Jesus spoke of physical birth. Jesus responded, "Unless one is born of water and the Spirit, he cannot enter into the kingdom of God."

Water baptism is but an outward symbol of the inward and powerful baptism of the Holy Spirit.

While it is tempting to think of "born of water" as a reference to physical birth, it has no support except in the modern mind. The Bible refers to physical birth as "born of blood," or "born of the will of man" (John 1:13). The text actually reads "born of water and spirit." The capitalization of the word "spirit" is unfortunate. There is no definite article before "spirit" in the original language and no reason to assume Jesus refers to the Holy Spirit until verse 8. The Greek word *pneuma* means "wind, breath, or spirit."

In verse 8 Jesus uses *pneuma* to refer to the wind. Jesus is contrasting the supernatural, heavenly elements of water and wind, which come from above, with earthly forces. Thus Jesus draws Nicodemus's attention away from physical birth to spiritual birth by analogy.[9] Spiritual birth is like the wind, in that you cannot see it but you witness its powerful effects.

Discovering a reference to baptism in Jesus' words to Nicodemus is more a case of finding what you are looking for than seeing what is there.

> And corresponding to that, baptism now saves you—not the removal of dirt from the flesh, but an appeal to God for a good conscience—through the resurrection of Jesus Christ. (1 Peter 3:21)

Why does Peter say, "baptism now saves you"? The key to the correct interpretation is to ask

what baptism Peter has in mind. How you answer this question governs what you believe about
salvation. It is not water baptism that saves, but
the baptism of the Spirit. The question, whether
or not baptism is necessary for regeneration, has
divided denominations. Although Peter mentions
water in the context, it is the water of Noah's flood.
The experience of Noah, during the flood that de-
stroyed the whole world, does not quite fit water
baptism. Noah did not even get wet. It was the
wicked who, in fact, received water baptism while
Noah and the seven others with him in the ark
were lifted safely above the waters of judgment.

It is clear that water baptism is not in Peter's
mind. He says that the kind of baptism that saves
you is "not the removal of dirt from the flesh."
What happens when you baptize a person in water? The water washes dirt off the flesh. Peter is
saying that no outward ritual can supply so great
a salvation. The power is not in the *ritual* but in
the *resurrection.* The word "answer" in the King
James Version can be translated "appeal or request." When we sincerely appeal to God for a
clean or good conscience, we are saved. Faith is
the appeal to God for a good conscience. It is the
request for His grace and forgiveness. Faith is
placing our trust in Christ to shelter us from the
wrath of divine justice, the way Noah did as he
entered the ark. Everyone who trusts this way in
Christ will be saved!

As stated above, the baptism that saves is the

baptism of the Holy Spirit. The moment an individual is made just in Christ, the Holy Spirit baptizes him or her into the body of Christ (1 Cor. 12:13). This baptism was what the prophet John predicted when he said, "I baptized you with water; but He will baptize you with the Holy Spirit" (Mark 1:8).

The baptism of the Holy Spirit is the great transforming act, changing people from the inside out. In it, the believer is identified with Christ in His death, burial, and resurrection. All the benefits of the new position come to the Christian in this baptism. "You in Me, and I in you" (John 14:20). No mere ceremony can do this. Water baptism is but an outward symbol of the inward and powerful baptism of the Holy Spirit. Water baptism pictures what has happened to us spiritually.

Texts Supposedly Relating Baptism to Washing

In one of Paul's testimonies of his conversion experience, he quotes Ananias as saying to him:

> And now why do you delay? Arise, and be baptized, and wash away your sins, calling on His name. (Acts 22:16)

The text seems to link baptism with the washing away of sins. Correct punctuation solves the problem. The two commands (imperatives) in the verse are "be baptized," and "wash away your sins." The Greek sentence structure divides into two parts. "As you arise, be baptized." The second part reads "and wash away your sins, calling on His name." Our sins are washed away as we call upon the name of Christ. This is the act of believing. Again, baptism follows as the outward demonstration of an inward faith.

Certainly, water baptism is closely linked to the conversion experience. It was a rite of entrance for Paul, who only three days before had seen Christ on the Damascus road. Still, the washing away of sins cannot be attributed to the act of baptism. As J. Oliver Buswell says, "It is by the atonement of Christ that sins are put away, and the metaphor of washing is entirely appropriate. It is the blood of Christ which cleanses us from all sin" (1 John 1:7).[10] However, this verse undeniably associates the act of baptism and a profession of faith.

> He saved us, not on the basis of deeds which we have done in righteousness, but according to His mercy, by the washing of regeneration and renewing by the Holy Spirit, whom He poured out upon us richly through Jesus Christ our Savior. (Titus 3:5–6)

The critical question is: What does Paul mean by the "washing of regeneration?" Advocates of baptismal regeneration tend to interpret "washing"

as a reference to water baptism that produces regeneration. There is no need to find water here
unless one is looking for it. Washing is a common
symbol for regeneration and the Holy Spirit's re-
newal. In 1 Cor. 6:11, washing is used in a figura-
tive way: "And such were some of you; but you were
washed, but you were sanctified, but you were justified in the name of the Lord Jesus Christ, and in
the Spirit of our God." In Ephesians, we find:

> Husbands, love your wives, just as Christ
> also loved the church and gave Himself
> up for her; that He might sanctify her,
> having cleansed her by the washing of
> water with the word. (Eph. 5:25–26)

Some interpret Paul here to mean that the
church is cleansed from sin by the waters of baptism. Such a view contradicts every other passage on the atonement. The word (*rhema*) here is
the term for "the preached or spoken word" as in
Ephesians 6:17. Regeneration is presented meta-
phorically as a cleansing in water when the gospel message is heard.

Even if water baptism is in the background of
the apostle's mind, as A. Skevington Wood suggests, "There is no hint of any mechanical view of
the sacrament, as if the mere application of water could in itself bring about the purification it
symbolizes. Nowhere does the New Testament

countenance baptismal regeneration in an *ex opere operato* sense."[11] The author of the epistle to the Hebrews writes:

> Let us draw near with a sincere heart in full assurance of faith, having our hearts sprinkled clean from an evil conscience and our bodies washed with pure water. Let us hold fast the confession of our hope without wavering, for He who promised is faithful. (Heb. 10:22–23)

This is an exhortation to draw near to God in prayer and worship. The context reminds us not to forsake the assembly of the saints together. Our assurance comes from clean hearts and washed bodies.

Although some have suggested it, the verse is hardly a proof-text for the Saturday night bath. While water baptism is probably what is being referred to, this text gives no support to baptismal regeneration. Instead, it contrasts the inner cleansing of the heart, which is sprinkled clean, with the outward symbol of that cleansing, the baptism of the body. Every other use of "sprinkled" or "sprinkling" in Hebrews involves blood, not water. Most likely the author of Hebrews expected us to understand that the blood of Christ has been sprinkled on our hearts to cleanse us from an evil conscience.

Evidence That Baptism Does Not Regenerate

The greatest evidence that baptism does not produce regeneration comes in the texts declaring that salvation, justification, cleansing, or regeneration derive from faith alone. The evidence that regeneration comes by faith alone is overwhelming. To believe baptismal regeneration is true, we must assume water baptism is to be added to every text about salvation. The following texts are samples of New Testament evidence:

But as many as received Him, to them He gave the right to become children of God, even to those who believe in His name. (John 1:12)

As Moses lifted up the serpent in the wilderness, even so must the Son of Man be lifted up; that whoever believes may in Him have eternal life. For God so loved the world, that He gave His only begotten Son, that whoever believes in Him should not perish, but have eternal life. (John 3:14–16)

He who believes in the Son has eternal life; but he who does not obey the Son shall not see life, but the wrath of God abides on him. (John 3:36)

Truly, truly, I say to you, he who believes has eternal life. (John 6:47)

[God] made no distinction between us and them [Jews and Gentiles], cleansing their hearts by faith. (Acts 15:9)

For this purpose I have appeared to you, to appoint you a minister and a witness . . . to open their eyes so that they [the Gentiles] may turn from darkness to light and from the dominion of Satan to God, in order that they may receive forgiveness of sins and an inheritance among those who have been sanctified by faith in Me. (Acts 26:16b–18)

This [display of Christ as a sacrifice for sin] was to demonstrate His righteousness, because in the forbearance of God He passed over the sins previously committed; for the demonstration, I say, of His righteousness at the present time, that He might be just and the justifier of the one who has faith in Jesus. Where then is the boasting? It is excluded. By what kind of law? Of works? No, but by a law of faith. For we maintain that a man is justified by faith apart from works of the Law. Or is God the God of Jews only? Is He not the

God of Gentiles also? Yes, of Gentiles also, since indeed God who will justify the circumcised by faith and the uncircumcised through faith is one. (Rom. 3:25b–30)

But to the one who does not work, but believes in Him who justifies the ungodly, his faith is reckoned as righteousness. (Rom. 4:5)

Therefore having been justified by faith, we have peace with God through our Lord Jesus Christ. (Rom. 5:1)

[We know] that a man is not justified by the works of the Law but through faith in Christ Jesus, even we have believed in Christ Jesus, that we may be justified by faith in Christ, and not by the works of the Law; since by the works of the Law shall no flesh be justified. (Gal. 2:16)

And the Scripture, foreseeing that God would justify the Gentiles by faith, preached the gospel beforehand to Abraham, saying, "All the nations shall be blessed in you." (Gal. 3:8)

The Law has become our tutor to lead us to Christ, that we may be justified by faith. (Gal. 3:24)

For by grace you have been saved through faith; and that not of yourselves, it is the gift of God; not as a result of works, that no one should boast. (Eph. 2:8–9)

I count all things to be loss in view of the surpassing value of knowing Christ Jesus my Lord, for whom I have suffered the loss of all things, and count them but rubbish in order that I may gain Christ, and may be found in Him, not having a righteousness of my own derived from the Law, but that which is through faith in Christ. (Phil. 3:8–9)

I found mercy, in order that in me as the foremost, Jesus Christ might demonstrate His perfect patience, as an example for those who would believe in Him for eternal life. (1 Tim. 1:16)

From childhood you have known the sacred writings which are able to give you the wisdom that leads to salvation through faith which is in Christ Jesus. (2 Tim. 3:15)

Though you have not seen Him, you love Him, and though you do not see Him now, but believe in Him, you greatly rejoice with joy inexpressible and full of glory, obtaining as the outcome of your faith the salvation of your souls. (1 Peter 1:8–9)

And this is His commandment, that we believe in the name of His Son Jesus Christ, and love one another, just as He commanded us. (1 John 3:23)

All these statements would be untrue, or at best would be only partially true, if baptism were an additional requirement for regeneration. One text actually separates water baptism from the gospel message. In 1 Corinthians 1:13–17, Paul writes:

Has Christ been divided? Paul was not crucified for you, was he? Or were you baptized in the name of Paul? I thank God that I baptized none of you except Crispus and Gaius, that no man should say you were baptized in my name. Now I did baptize also the household of Stephanas; beyond that, I do not know whether I baptized any other. For Christ did not send me to baptize, but to preach the gospel, not in cleverness of speech, that the cross of Christ should not be made void.

If water baptism were an essential part of salvation, then Paul would have included it as part of his commission. If water baptism itself had saving significance, then why would Paul distinguish it from preaching the gospel? If baptism were an essential requirement for salvation, should Paul not have included it with the gospel? Theologically, baptism is not a requirement, but practically, it was the New Testament way of expressing faith. Probably that is the source of the confusion.

Finally, Peter's ministry in Caesarea, recorded in Acts 10:44–48a, demonstrates the relationship between regeneration and water baptism:

> While Peter was still speaking these words, the Holy Spirit fell upon all those who were listening to the message. And all the circumcised believers who had come with Peter were amazed, because the gift of the Holy Spirit had been poured out upon the Gentiles also. For they were hearing them speaking with tongues and exalting God. Then Peter answered, "Surely no one can refuse the water for these to be baptized who have received the Holy Spirit just as we did, can he?" And he ordered them to be baptized in the name of Jesus Christ.

The Holy Spirit fell in sovereign regeneration and Spirit baptism upon these Gentiles as they heard the Word. The Spirit placed them within the body of Christ in an instant, granting them new life and good consciences because of their faith. The evidence that God had accepted these Gentiles as full members of the body was so overwhelming that the Jewish delegation agreed they could properly administer water baptism. The people had already been saved by the Spirit. Water baptism was the outward sign of their inward transformation.

This does not demean water baptism as useless or unimportant. It is the God-ordained means by which faith in Christ is expressed. However, it is not a saving rite. The baptism that saves is the baptism of the Holy Spirit.

Endnotes

Chapter 1

1. J. D. Douglas, ed., *The New Bible Dictionary* (London: InterVarsity, 1962), s.v. "Baptism."

Chapter 2

1. Paul K. Jewett, "Baptism," in Merrill C. Tenney, ed., *Zondervan Pictorial Bible Encyclopedia* (Grand Rapids: Zondervan, 1988), 466.
2. Ibid.
3. J. D. Douglas, ed., *The New Bible Dictionary* (London: InterVarsity, 1962), s.v. "Baptism."
4. Everett F. Harrison, Geoffrey W. Bromiley,

and Carl F. H. Henry, eds., *Baker's Dictionary of Theology* (Grand Rapids: Baker, 1960), s.v. "Sacrament."

5. H. Wayne House, "Baptism for the Forgiveness of Sins," part 1, *Christian Research Journal* 22, no. 2: 29.

6. Ibid.

7. "The Orthodox Faith," Rainbow Series 2: Worship (Orthodox Church in America website, 2000).

8. Paul Enns, "Ecclesiology: Doctrine of the Church," in *The Moody Handbook of Theology* (Chicago: Moody, 1989), 363.

9. Millard J. Erickson, *Christian Theology*, 2d ed. (Grand Rapids: Baker, 1999), 1102.

Chapter 3

1. Marty Zide, missionary with the Midwest Messianic Center, St. Louis, Missouri, interview with author, July 1998. Used with permission.

2. Soman Varghese, interview with author, February 2000. Used with permission.

Chapter 4

1. Walter Bauer, Wilbur F. Gingrich, and Frederick W. Danker, *A Greek-English Lexicon of the New Testament and Other Early Christian Literature*, 2d ed., rev. F. W. Gingrich and F. W. Danker (Chicago: University of Chicago Press, 1979).

2. Yohanan Aharoni and Michael Avi-Yonah, *The Macmillan Bible Atlas* (New York: Macmillan, 1968), 241.

3. Johannes P. Louw and Eugene A. Nida, *Greek-English Lexicon of the New Testament, Based on Semantic Domains* (New York: United Bible Societies, 1989).

4. Charles C. Ryrie, *Basic Theology* (Wheaton, Ill.: Victory, 1986), 424.

Chapter 6

1. Everett F. Harrison, Geoffrey W. Bromiley, and Carl F. H. Henry, eds., *Baker's Dictionary of Theology* (Grand Rapids: Baker, 1960), s.v. "Baptism, Infant."

2. Paul J. Achtemeier, ed., *Harper's Bible Dictionary* (San Francisco: Harper and Row, 1985).

3. Paul K. Jewett, "Baptism," in Merrill C. Tenney, ed., *Zondervan Pictorial Bible Encyclopedia* (Grand Rapids: Zondervan, 1988), 467.

4. Millard J. Erickson, *Christian Theology*, 2d ed. (Grand Rapids: Baker, 1999), 1103.

5. Jewett, "Baptism," 467.

6. Ibid.

7. Harrison, Bromiley, and Henry, "Baptism, Infant," 87.

8. John Walvoord and Roy Zuck, eds., *The Bible Knowledge Commentary New Testament* (Wheaton, Ill.: Victor, 1984), 359.

9. Zane Hodges, lecture notes, "The Gospel
    of John" (unpub., Dallas Theological Semi-
    nary, 1976).

10. J. Oliver Buswell, *A Systematic Theology
    of the Christian Religion* (Grand Rapids:
    Zondervan 1976), 253.

11. A. Skevington Wood, "Ephesians," in
    Frank E. Gaebelein, ed., *The Expositor's
    Bible Commentary* (Grand Rapids:
    Zondervan, 1978), 77.